The Funny Thing About a Last Will

Donna Broom, J.D.

Copyright © 2013 Donna Broom, J.D.

All rights reserved.

ISBN:1493799053
ISBN-13:978-1493799053

Library of Congress Control Number: 2014900187

DEDICATION

This book is possible because of the love and support of my husband who is my inspiration, my friend and partner. In addition, special thanks to my three sons, who put up with the many hours of writing that had to go into getting this book finished.

The Funny Thing About a Will

CONTENTS

1	Introduction	1
2	Strange Requests	3
3	Non-Proper Documentation	46
4	To My Pets	51
5	Revenge and Last Words	59
6	Ignored Last Wishes	64
7	Oops, I Forgot	68
8	Battle for the Estate	78
9	Afterword	85

1 INTRODUCTION

The last wishes of others have always intrigued me. I have often wondered about the first estate plan. Did Adam and Eve die with a Will? God left them all the plants and the animals on the earth to do as they so wished. How did they split that up amongst their heirs? Was Cain to be the first disinherited heir?

My mother's Will was the first I had ever read. She died when I was eleven and it was not until the age of seventeen that I was able to find her Last Will at the county courthouse. My mom was one of the most creative women I have ever known and I had a belief that this document would pour forth her creative personality. I imagined that there would be a last message of love for her children.

I was disappointed. Her Will was nothing special to read, it was a standard document, which stated, "I leave everything to my husband and if he is dead, I leave it to my kids." There were pages and pages of standard language appointing an executor, listing the duties of the executor, and a "no contest clause." At 17, I had no understanding of terms such as provisions, statutory requirements, "no contest clause" and execution rules. I learned later that people generally do not include special provisions or last statements.

A few years later, I attended law school, and learned that there were many types of standard Wills. I also learned that people did have desires they wished expressed and that each Will has to be tailor made to fit every person. After twelve years of practicing probate and estate plan law, I have drafted more Wills than I can remember and seen countless others. My fascination of Wills has continued as a hobby.

I started this book as a weekly column on my website. As I researched more Last Wills, I found some strange estate plans. I began collecting the stories. One day, my husband found my file and looked at the mountain of information and mentioned, "You know there is enough here to fill a book."

He was right. The hardest part was taking all the information and organizing it into categories. Once I started, the facts wrote themselves. What follows is labor of love, in no way can this book contain all examples of strange in the world of Last Wills and Testaments, but I hope you enjoy the collection and laugh a little.

2 STRANGE REQUESTS

We all imagine making an outlandish request in our Will, a portion of our estate to go to a charity, leave something behind to a person who touched our lives or having one last party with our friends and love ones. Imagine receiving an invitation to the dissection of a loved one. You read that it was his last request, as stated in his Last Will. People are superstitious about death and have strange ideas of what they wish done with bodies. The Will serves the purpose of allowing a person to leave property and their bodies in a manner of their choosing.

Margaret Allen

When Margaret and her husband settled in the village of Solva in West Wales, the residents made them both feel at home in the community. When her husband died, the residents gave support to Margaret and helped see her though a rough time. After her own death, Margaret's Will revealed how grateful she was for everything bestowed on her by the residents.

The document stated that she wished to use £5,000 of her estate, to pay for a Christmas dinner at a local hotel for all of the residents of Solva. In addition, her Will also left a £500 gift to all those residents who were over the age of 60, and had lived in the village of Solva for more than twenty years.

Earl Allen
Died 1925

A Texas man feared waking up to find himself buried alive. He requested a working telephone placed in his hand, in the coffin. His theory was that if there had been a mistake made and he was still alive he would call for help. In today's modern world, with the help of a cell phone that request would be easy. However, in 1924, all phones required a working line. His Will stipulated that a disconnection could occur two days after his burial with no calls.

Fredric Baur

June 14, 1918 – May 4, 2008

Fredric Baur was an educated chemist who had developed new fry oils, to use in the kitchen, and freeze-dried ice cream. His biggest claim to fame was as the inventor of the Pringles can. The tube that stores those curved shaped potato chips that are hard to stop eating.

Upon his death, Baur requested his remains be cremated and some of his ashes be buried in a Pringles can. He told his children he wished to share his eternal rest with his invention. When he died in 2008, his children honored his request by taking his cremated ashes and purchasing a can of Pringles Original at a local pharmacy. They placed part of his remains in the can for burial. The rest of his ashes were split into two places. An urn holds most of his remains, but a relative received a small portion, as well.

Golda Bechal

Died 2001

At the age of 70, Ms. Bechal changed her Will naming Kim Sing Man and Bee Lian Man to receive a gift of £10,000,000. Sing and Bee Lian were the owners of a local Chinese restaurant where Bechal was a frequent guest. The new Will disinherited Bechal's closest relatives, which consisted of nieces and nephews.

Those relatives did contest the Will claiming that Bechal had dementia and was not of sound mind in the new Will. After a three-year court battle, the judge found that the Will was valid. Bechal had understanding of her financial worth and therefore was of sound mind.

Jack Benny

February 14 1894 – December 26, 1974

Jack Benny was an American comedian. He got his start in vaudeville, and then made the transition over to radio and television. He was a recognized violinist and preformed his comedy on stage with a violin in his hand. He died December 26, 1974. George Burns, who was Benny's best friend of fifty years, attempted to deliver his eulogy but sorrow overtook him and he could not finish.

Benny's Will left a hefty sum of money to a local florist for the sole purpose of delivering one long stemmed rose a day to Benny's wife for the rest of her life. She would die nine years later and her estate estimates that she had received approximately 3,000 roses.

Jeremy Bentham

February 15, 1748 – June 6, 1832

Bentham led a life dedicated to the philosophy of law and social reform. Bentham wished, after his death, his body dissected and preserved in a wooden box that he named the Auto-Icon. During the months leading up to his death, Bentham prepared for such an undertaking. Two days after Bentham's death, a small group of select friends traveled to hear a lecture over the remains, and then witnessed his dissection.

The doctor preforming the dissection removed the head and skeleton for chemical preservation. Doctors then used hay to stuff the skeleton in order to shape a body under clothes. However, the head, which had to undertake a mummification process, took on a strange appearance. The skin darkened and stretched over the skull. Eventually a wax replica replaced the head, since many found the mummified piece scary.

Edgar Bergen

February 16, 1903 – September 30, 1978

Edgar Bergen had built a ventriloquist entertainment career with his dummy partner, Charlie McCarthy. They performed up to the time of Bergen's death. The Smithsonian Institute inherited Charlie. However, in his Will, Edgar donated $10,000 to the Actor's Fund of America to create the Charlie McCarthy Fund. The fund would put on benefits for hospitals and the underprivileged. The only requirement would be that ventriloquist use Charlie McCarthy as the dummy.

Napoleon Bonaparte

August 15, 1769 – May 5, 1821,

Napoleon was Emperor of France and conqueror of a majority of Europe. He was eventually defeated, and exiled to an island off the coast of Africa until his death. Originally, historians theorize that stomach cancer claimed his life, since Napoleon's father died of the same sickness.

After his death, Napoleon wished for his head shaved and his hair divided amongst his friends. At the time, a popular poison was arsenic, which was undetectable if ingested over a long period. The hair holds the true signs of the poison. It was his wish to have his friends investigate his death and if anyone found that poison was a cause of his demise, they would avenge him.

John Bowman
January 16, 1816 – September 18, 1891

Born in Vermont, Mr. Bowman found his fortune in the business of tanning hide. His two daughters and his beloved wife passed away before him, and he purchased land to build a Greek style marble mausoleum. Bowman planned every detail of their final resting place. He oversaw construction of a mansion across the street from the mausoleum, and even had a plan in case they all decided to return.

In his last Will, a trust would set aside $50,000 from the estate to pay for servants who would maintain the twenty-one room house, and prepare a dinner every night, in case the Bowman's ever wished to return. Performance of these actions occurred until the trust ran out of money in 1950.

Today, the Laurel Glen Cemetery Association preserves the mausoleum, known as Laurel Glen, and the mansion, Laurel Hall, as tourist attractions in Vermont. People can see a life size statue of John Bowman carrying a laurel at the grave.

Henry Budd
Died 1862

Henry Budd was not too keen on the fashion trend of growing moustaches. In his last will and testament, he left his sons a trust funded with £200,000, which they could access under the provision they would never grow a moustache of their own.

Luis Carlos de Noronha Cabral da Camara

A wealthy Portuguese man, Camara, set into motion an estate that named seventy strangers as heirs. After his death, it was hard to convince the named heirs that they had actually inherited the money. Many of the named thought it was a scam.

Andre Carnegie

November 25, 1835 – August 11, 1919

Andrew Carnegie was an American industrialist who led the way for modern construction with his company, Carnegie Steel. He was one of the three richest men in the world. In 1901, Carnegie was thinking of retiring and fellow industrialist J.P. Morgan made an offer to purchase his company to for $480 million, the equivalent of 13 billion by today's standards.

After the sale, Carnegie began a life of philanthropy that would see him give away as much as he could during his life. At the time of his death all that remained was $30,000,000, ten million, of which the estate divided among charities and foundations. The Carnegie Corporation inherited the remaining twenty million. In his Will, Carnegie left little to his wife and daughter.

In a provision of his Will he stated, "Having years ago made provisions for my wife beyond her desires and ample to enable for her to provide for our beloved daughter, Margaret; and being unable to judge at present what provisions for our daughter will best promote her happiness, leave to her mother the duty of providing for her as her mother deems best. A mother's love will be the best guide."

Carnegie had already set up trusts in the name of his wife and daughter while he was still alive so they would not have to worry.

Carnegie also set up annuities to certain named officials to allow them a comfortable retirement:

President Taft would receive $10,000 a year.

Hon. John Burns would receive $5000 a year.

Viscount Morley would receive $10,000 a year.

The widow of Grover Cleveland would receive $5,000 a year.

Mrs. Theodore Roosevelt would receive $5,000 a year.

David Lloyd George would receive $10,000 a year.

Thomas Burt, M.P. would receive $5,000 a year.

John Wilson, M.P. would receive $5,000 a year.

Walter Damrosch would receive $3,000 a year.

Conrad Cantzen

Died 1945

American actor, Cantzen died and left his estate, valued at around $200,000 dollars to the Actors Fund. The sole purpose of the estate was to establish the Conrad Cantzen Shoe Fund. The fund dedicated time and resources to provide shoes to working actors. Cantzen believed that a good pair of shoes would make a great first impression to any director. The fund is still active today vowing to reimburse up to forty dollars, for a pair of shoes costing no more than a hundred dollars to any unemployed actor

Marie Curie
November 7, 1867 – July 4, 1934

Marie Curie, became famous for her research into radioactivity. She coined the phrase 'theory of radioactivity,' and developed techniques for isolating isotope. She discovered two new elements on the periodic table, polonium and radium.

Curie had the distinguished honor of winning two Nobel prizes, the first in 1906, the Nobel Prize for physics. She shared the award with fellow chemist Henri Becquerel and her husband Pierre Curie. The second in 1911 for her work in chemistry. She is the only person to win the Nobel Prize in two different fields of science.

In 1934, her work, literally, killed her. She died from aplastic anemia. Her bone marrow could no longer produce healthy blood cells. All the years of exposure to radiation brought on her sickness.

Because of the dangerous material she worked with her notes dated back to 1890, to this day, are too dangerous to handle due to the extreme levels of radiation, and considered a hazardous material. After her death, the only real asset in her estate was a gram of pure radium, a gift from the women of America.

Her Will stated, "The value of the element being too great to transfer to a personal heritage, I desire to will the gram of radium to the University of Paris on the condition that my daughter, Irene Curie, shall have entire liberty to use this gram."

The element named Curium, chosen to represent the 96th element on the periodic table of elements, honors both Marie and her husband.

Henry Durrell

Will executed 1921

Henry Durrell was a Bermuda tycoon who died with no children of his own. However, he did have three nephews that he cared for equally. Durrell's quandary was how to leave the estate so no one would get their feelings hurt. His answer was to have them roll the dice and the winner takes all. Richard Durrell emerged the victorious winner of the estate, including a lavish house in Bermuda.

Bob Fosse

June 23, 1923 – September 23, 1987

Bob Fosse was an American entertainer who worked as an actor, dancer, choreographer, and director. He won the academy award for direction, for the film version of "Cabaret." His Will called for a grand dinner after his death. Sixty-six artists, writers, entertainers and other people who had been kind to him during his life, received $25,000 so they could all "go out and have diner on me." Some of the recipients were Neil Simon, Melanie Griffith, Liza Minnelli and Roy Scheider.

Matthias Flemming

Died 1869

Flemming left his employees £10 each in his Will, however those with moustaches received half that amount.

Benjamin Franklin

January 16, 1706 – April 17, 1790.

Benjamin Franklin is the quintessential essence of what defines a Renaissance man. Franklin was an inventor, scientist, political activist, and postmaster. His pivotal role in the American Revolution helped secure aid from France, which facilitated our freedom from British rule. When Franklin died, 20,000 people attended his funeral. His final resting place is in Philadelphia.

In his Will, Franklin set aside $4,400 in a trusts for his hometown city of Boston, and another $4,400 in a trust for his adopted home of Philadelphia. The trusts were to sit and accrue interest for two hundred years and the money be spent for the betterment of the cities and their citizens. By 1990, nearly $2,000,000 was in the Philadelphia trust and the city used the money for mortgage loans to their citizens. The Boston trust had grown to $5,000,000 and the city put the money to fund scholarships for local high school students and The Franklin Institute of Technology.

Mr. Franklin also expressed a request in his Will that his daughter not take part in "the expensive, vain and useless pastime of wearing jewels." However, this request came after he had received a portrait of the King of France with a frame that contained four hundred and eight diamonds. This picture had been a gift for the time he served as the American Ambassador to France.

Tony Gribble

After his death, Gribble requested his heirs place his ashes into an egg timer so he could continue to help around the house.

Mark Gruenwald

June 18, 1953 – August 12, 1996

Mark Gruenwald was born June 18, 1953. He worked in the comic book industry, notably Marvel Comics. He has worked on the comic book titles associated with The Avengers, Iron Man, Thor and Spider Woman. His work on Captain America helped to create the characters, U.S. Agent, Diamondback, and Crossbones.

Gruenwald died on August 12, 1996, from a heart attack. In his Will, he stipulated that his remains be cremated and his ashes mixed into ink, then used to create a comic book. A Squadron Supreme comic compilation, another comic he helped create, were issued with the ashes of its creator.

The Funny Thing About a Will

E.J. Halley

Halley might not have been in a sound mind when he created his Will. He would list people who had treated him well in his life leaving them various sums of money. His family contested the will after reading he left the cook at the hospital, "who took the snakes out of my broth," $5,000 dollars. In addition, he left another $5,000 to the nurse who got rid of "the pink monkey that was in my bed."

"Steady" Ed Headrick
June 28, 1924 – August 12, 2002

Fans of Disc golf regard "Steady" Ed Headrick as the sports creator. He helped do so much for the sport, having invented the first course, goal and special discs. He gave his idea to the public domain so it would grow.

After his death, Headrick wished for his heirs to cremate his remains and then mold them into a limited number of flying discs. The commemorative disks gave joy to friends and family members with a few used to raise funds for charity.

William Randolph Hearst

April 29, 1863 – August 14, 1951

Considered by some to be the inventor of modern journalism, Hearst created the world's largest newspaper chain. While in his twenty's, he took charge of the San Francisco Examiner, a newspaper purchased by his father. He brought in the best equipment and stole the best writers from other papers.

Hearst also went on to serve two terms in the United States House of Representatives, but was defeated in a run for the mayoral race of New York. Hearst married in 1903, to Millicent Veronica Wilson, who bore him five sons over the years. Hearst grew apart from his wife but they never divorced. He began an affair with actress, Marion Davies.

Hearst died in 1951, and left behind a vast estate of land, money, an art collection, and a castle in California. All estimated to be worth around $58,000,000. He stated in his Will that anyone who could prove, "that he or she is a child of mine…the sum of one dollar. I hereby declare that any such asserted claim . . . would be utterly false."

The actual document was as thick as a book, he asked to

leave his castle to the University of California, but the college, seeing the property as too expensive to maintain, rejected this gift. The State of California took transfer of the property and now opens the castle for public tours.

The estate was broken up into three trusts one for his wife, one for his children and the last being The William Randolph Hearst Foundation, which took 75% of the Estate.

Patrick Henry
May 29, 1763- June 6, 1799

Patrick Henry was one of the original patriots that fought for American independence, most famously known for the "Give me Liberty or Give me Death," speech. Henry married his first wife and together had six kids. After her death, he remarried and proceeded to produce eleven more children.

In his Will he left his entire estate to his wife with the stipulation that she never remarry, stating "it would make me unhappy to feel I have worked all my life only to support another man's wife." However, The wife did remarry Henry's cousin, who was also named executor of Henry's estate.

Dr. Sophie Herzog

1848 -1925

The first woman surgeon in Texas wanted her family to bury her wearing what she called her "Slug Necklace." The neck charm was composed of 27 bullets that she had extracted from other people all held together with gold links. She had prided herself on her surgical bullet extraction.

Harry Houdini

March 24, 1874 – October 31, 1926

Most people consider Harry Houdini one of the greatest escape artists and magicians of all time. He was born, Erik Weisz in Budapest, Austria-Hungry, on March 24, 1874. Houdini immigrated, with his family to the United States in 1878.

Houdini began his magic career in 1891 and rose to fame. When he became the president of the Society of American Magicians, he began a crusade to uphold professional standards and expose frauds.

He dedicated the last few years of his life debunking mediums, psychics and spiritualist. Those people who claim to be able to talk to the dead, for a price.

When Houdini died on October 31, 1926, he had a certain codicil in his Will. If it were possible to communicate after death, Houdini would try. His wife would hold a séance once a year to try to communicate with the departed magician, where upon he would convey a secret code to his wife, to let her know that it was truly him. For ten years, she held the séance on the anniversary of his death, and for ten years failed to contact Houdini. The wife quit holding the event stating, "ten years is long enough to wait for any man."

Today, many magicians throughout the world continue the tradition of holding the séance.

Sam Houston

March 2, 1793 – July 26, 1863

Sam Houston was the leader of the A1rmy of Texas in the war against Mexico. Houston left special instruction in his Will for the education of his sons.

"My will is that my sons should receive solid and useful education, and that no portion of their time may be devoted to the study of abstract sciences. I greatly desire that they may possess a thorough knowledge of the English language with a good knowledge of the Latin language. I also request that they be instructed in the knowledge of the Holy Scriptures; and next to these that they be rendered thorough in knowledge of geography and history. I wish my sons early taught an utter contempt for novels and light reading. In all that pertains to my sons I wish particular regard paid to their morals as well as character and morals of those whom they may be associated or instructed."

Ben Johnson

June 11 1572 – August 6, 1637

Ben Johnson was a playwright, and poet. He had written plays and cast William Shakespeare as an actor. His last request was to have a grave in Westminster abbey, but he could not afford such a burial. The church made a deal that Johnson could have space in the church in an upright, eighteen square inch, grave. Later the grave would be marked with the inscription "O Rare Ben Johnson" translated "Pray for Ben Johnson"

Janis Joplin

January 19, 1943 – October 4 1970

Born in Port Arthur Texas, Joplin became a voice of the 1960's. She battled drugs and alcohol her entire career. In 1970, she failed to make an appearance at a recording studio and the local authorities discovered her body in a hotel room. The official cause ruled as an overdose of heroin, mixed with alcohol.

Only two days before her death she had revised her Will, asking that an all-night party be thrown in her honor. The Party invited two hundred guests to her favorite pub, and $2,500 to pay the tab "so my friends can get blasted after I'm gone."

John B. Kelley

October 4, 1889 – June 20, 1960

John B. Kelly was a triple Olympic gold medal winner and one of the most gifted athletes in the sport of rowing. More notably, he was the father of actress Grace Kelley. Kelley earned a fortune in contracting and construction. When his daughter was to marry the prince of Monaco, he paid a $2,000,000 dollar dowry for the wedding.

In his Will, he attempted to have one last laugh with his children. To his son he left all his personal possessions: trophies, jewelry, and clothing. All except the items, that son had already stolen from his father. Kelley found it unnecessary to give him something that his son had already taken possession.

To his son-in-law, the Prince of Monaco, he left nothing hoping that the money he leaves his daughter will help prevent her from bankrupting the principality with her dress bill

James Kidd

Born July 18, 1879

Missing 1949

Pronounced dead 1954

James Kidd was born in New York, and moved to Arizona in 1918. He worked for the local copper company and owned many mines of his own. Including what he believed was a Haunted mine.

On December 29, 1949, local authorities issued a missing person report for Kidd. With no relatives and few friends, his absence took a while for anyone to notice. Authorities then proceeded to issue a declaration of death in 1954. His safety deposit box opened in 1957, and the rest of his estate finally dealt with in 1967.

Mr. Kidd had managed to create a small fortune, $175,000 and left behind a valid Will. He declared that his money would go toward research of some scientific proof of a spirit outside of the body. Court filings overwhelmed the courthouse, of people and organizations claiming to have proof of the spirit or soul.

In 1970, the funds had grown in value to $500,000 and the court finally dispensed with two-thirds going to the American Society for Physical Research, and the Physical Research Foundation.

Audrey Knauer
Died 1997

Most people have heard of leaving sums or money to charities or government facilities. Then there are people who leave money to celebrities, even though they have never met each other. Ms. Knauer Died in 1997 and she stipulated in her Will that the sum of $300,000 to go to actor Charles Bronson. Bronson actually accepted $150,000 of the fund, which he donated to charity. Her Will then stipulated any money not accepted by Mr. Bronson should go to the local library, and her family would receive nothing.

Charles Vance Miller

1853-1926

Charles Vance Miller was a lover of practical jokes involving people's greed. In life, he would leave money on the sidewalk and hide watching passersby hurry to try and to pocket it.

After his death, his Estate set up a contest called 'The Stork Derby.' His Will stipulated that a large sum of money would go to any Toronto woman who could produce the most offspring in the decade after his death. Four women would emerged as winners with nine children each, all taking home around $125,000

However, that was not the end of his jokes. He also stipulated that three men, all of whom hated the other, a joint lifetime tenancy in Millers vacation home located in Jamaica. He left $700,000 in stock in an alcohol company to protestant ministers and leaders of the prohibition movement. They could have access to the funds as long they helped in the running of the company and drew dividends on the stock. Finally, he requested his estate leave $25,000 of Jockey Club Stock, (horse races) to an anti-horse-racing advocate.

He considered his Will to be his final and greatest prank stating,

"This will is necessarily uncommon and capricious because I have no dependents or near relations and no duty rests upon me to leave any property at my death and what I do leave is proof of my folly in gathering and retaining more that I required in life."

Of course, distant relatives tried to invalidate the document, but Miller had constructed such an elegant Will that it survived ten years of litigation and paid out the prize money to all the winners of the stork derby. The story even had enough merit to inspire a movie in 2002 titled "The Stork Derby."

Robert Millar

Robert Millar despised traffic and thought the main cause of traffic to be motorists who double-parked. In his Will, he left $5000 to the officer who would write the most ticket for double parking.

George Orwell

June 25, 1903 – January 21, 1950

George Orwell wrote many modern masterpieces such as

Nineteen Eighty-Four and Animal Farm. However, do not spend much time looking for his grave marker. In his Last Will, Orwell asked his grave to carry his real name, Eric Arthur Blair.

Sir Walter Raleigh

1554 – October 29 1618

Sir Walter Raleigh was one of the first explores of the new world from England. He helped to establish the Virginia colony. Raleigh was also responsible for the popular spread of the tobacco in Europe.

For his attack on the Spanish, he was to be executed by having his head cleaved from his body. However, he made requests in his Will. He wished that everyone who smokes attend his funeral, and all attendees be given ten pounds of tobacco and a pipe with the name Raleigh on it. He wished for his coffin to have barrels of tobacco at his feet and his favorite pipe and a box of matches at his side.

Armand Jean Du Plessis, Cardinal- Duc de Richelieu et de Fronsac

Also known as Cardinal Richelieu

September 9, 1585 – December 4, 1642

Cardinal Richelieu was a man that would find later fame in the fictional work of Alexander Dumas' The Three Musketeers. The real man was not as evil as the character that Dumas wrote about in the book. However, he did possess a keen political mind that rivaled Makaveli himself. He helped the king of France in the war on England. At the same time, he amassed a great fortune.

In his Will he left 1.5 million Livres, the main currency, to King Louis XIII. He wished his remaining estate split amongst his niece and nephews. His books were given to one nephew as long as he pays a minimum 400 Livres yearly for a cleaning service to sweep daily and clean the books.

Gene Roddenberry

August 19, 1921 – October 24, 1991

The creator of the Star Trek series was born on August 19, 1921, in El Paso, Texas. During his life he created an empire of television shows and movies that have enthralled the people of all generations. His legacy continued with the recent release of the blockbuster movie Star Trek: Into the Darkness.

Roddenberry died on October 24, 1991, his Will stipulated that a satellite in orbit would spread his ashes around the earth.

In 1992, a part of Roddenberry's ashes flew into space aboard the Space Shuttle Columbia. Then in 1997 a spacecraft carried, more of Roddenberry's ashes along with other peoples remain into space, in 2002 due to orbit decay the spacecraft fell back to earth and disintegrated on reentry.

Another space flight would carry the ashes of Roddenberry and his wife's ashes into space for the final frontier in 2014.

Ayn Rand

February 2, 1905 – March 6, 1982

Rand was a famous author spreading the world of capitalism through such books as The Fountainhead and Atlas Shrugged. In life, she wore a dollar sign broach on her lapel. In death, she requested a six-foot dollar sign floral arrangement placed next to her coffin at her funeral.

Donel Russell

Donel Russell found a special way to immortalize himself. In his Will, he requested that a tanner would remove the skin from his dead body, and then used to bind a collection of his complete works.

The Mortuary workers refused to perform the request. The widow went to the courts to uphold the Last Will. However, the courts decided that the request violated the laws about the disposal of human remains.

Marquis de Sade

June 2, 1740 – December 2, 1814

The Marquis was a French Aristocrat and political revolutionary. He left instructions in his Will that no one was to cut open his body for any reason. In addition, it would remain for two days in the room in which he died. At the end of such time, the coffin would be nailed shut and properly buried.

Solomon Sandborn

Died 1871

Considered a true American patriot, Solomon Sandborn wanted to leave his mark on American history. Originally, a hat maker from Massachusetts, his heirs discovered, after his death that Sandborn wished for a friend to make two drums using the skin of his body. One drum was to have written on it the Declaration of Independence and the other the Popes Universal Prayer.

The drums were then to play Yankee Doodle Dandy at sunrise on June 17th at Bunker Hill, the anniversary of The Battle of Bunker Hill.

William Shakespeare

April 26, 1564 – April 23, 1616

To understand the works of Shakespeare is to have understanding of a different language. His words fill our minds with misdirection saying one thing and at the same time meaning another. His Last Will and Testament is no different. Shakespeare married Anne Hathaway (not the modern actress) and with her Shakespeare had three children, Susanna and a set of twins, a son Hammet and a daughter Judith. Hammet died at the age of 11. Scholars know little of why he left his family for London, but this is where he began his great career as a playwright.

In his Will, he left the bulk of his estate to his eldest daughter Susanna, in terms that she is to pass it down intact to the "first son of her body," which was the way in England to pass on an estate with only female heirs. Shakespeare mentions his wife Anne in a little scribble at the end of the document, leaving her "his second best bed." This statement has scholars confused, even today. Whether this statement is an insult to his wife, and this was his way of telling her that he loved another. Others consider the second bed to be the marital bed and this showed how he always loved her. However, it could literally mean his second bed, seeing how a good bed free of disease and vermin was such a rare treasure and hard to find.

Shakespeare also took special care to note what he wanted on his grave marker, he always had a flare for magic and the occult in his writings. He had a written a curse to be placed on his tombstone to scare grave robbers.

(MODERN TRANSLATION)

Good Friend, for Jesus' sake forbear

To dig the dust enclosed here

Blessed be the man that spares these stones

And cursed be he that moves my bones

This curse has proven to be effective to ward off grave robbers and others. When his wife died, seven years later, the gravediggers where scared to dig the grave so her body could be buried on top of his, which was the custom at the time. Even today, people, such as workers, are still wary of disturbing the site. While preforming a restoration on the church in 2008, Shakespeare's grave was not disturbed.

George Bernard Shaw

July 26, 1856 – November 2, 1950

Born in Ireland, Shaw became famous for his literary works, most notably Pygmalion, The Apple Cart and Saint Joan. Over his life, Mr. Shaw had written about different political systems and religions, showing their effect on the world. He won the Nobel Prize for Literature in 1925, but refused the monetary award, instead asking that the funds be used to translate the works of August Strindberg from Swedish to English. He also received an Oscar in 1938 for the film adaptation of his play Pygmalion, in which he wrote the dialog.

In his last Will and Testament, Mr. Shaw stated, "religious convictions and scientific views cannot at present be more specifically defined than as those of a believer in Creative Evolution." He stated in his Will that he was a firm believer in Darwin's theory of Evolution. He asked no one to imply that he believed in any religion. In addition, that no item should, "take the form of a cross or any other instrument of torture or symbol of blood sacrifice. "

He asked that his heirs use the bulk of his estate to promote a new 40 symbol phonic alphabet of his own creation. Unfortunately, the courts overruled his request, indicating it as an impossible task, and then divided his estate between The British Museum, The National Gallery of Ireland, and The Royal Academy of Dramatic Art.

Robert Louis Stevenson

November 13, 1850 – December 3, 1894

Creator of such works as Treasure Island, Kidnapped and the Strange Case of Dr. Jekyll and Mr. Hyde, he is one of the most translated authors of all time. He traveled the world extensively and in his later years purchased land on the island of Upolo, Samoa. On a cold December, while speaking to his wife, he exclaimed, "What's that, does my face look strange," and fell to the floor. Stevenson died a few hours later.

In life, Stevenson made friends with Mrs. Anne H. Ide, who possessed a birthday that fell upon Christmas day. She had spoken with Stevenson about always feeling cheated out of a real birthday. In his Last Will and Testament, Stevenson had left his birthday, November 13 to Ms. Ide so she would have a proper birthday.

His family buried Stevenson overlooking the sea, and as one final request wished for one of his poems inscribed on his grave marker.

Under the wide and starry sky,

Dig the grave and let me lie.

Glad did I live and gladly die,

And I laid me down with a will.

This be the verse you grave for me:

Here he lies where he longed to be;

Home is the sailor, home from sea,

And the hunter home from the hill

Hunter S. Thompson

July 18, 1937 – February 20, 2005

Noted reporter and author of Fear and Loathing in Las Vegas, Thompson wished to "impregnate" the sky with his remains. His ashes were loaded up into fireworks and exploded above the heads of the attendees of his service. In all likely hood, the attendees also breathed in little pieces of him as well.

Sandra West

January 2, 1939 – March 10, 1977

West lived her life as a Beverly Hills socialite all paid for by being a Texas oil heir. When she died, she left her brother-in-law $3 million dollars, on the condition that he would bury her wearing a lacy nightgown and seated in her favorite powder blue Ferrari with the seat set at a "Comfortable" angle. The brother-in-law, Sol West, tried to find another way around the Will, but in the end if he wanted his money he would have to uphold the request. In a box measuring 6 feet by 8 feet by 17 feet, he laid then the body, and the car to rest. The box was place in a nine foot deep hole then covered with concrete.

Harold West

Died 1972

In life, West did not fear death as much as retuning as one of the Undead. Vampires haunted the life of West and fear of returning to life as a bloodsucker consumed him. He left instructions for his burial after his death, "My doctor is to drive a steel stake though my heart to make sure that I am properly dead."

Paula Yates

April 24, 1959 – September 17, 2000

Yates was a British entertainment personality. She spent her whole life fighting addiction to drugs. She lost her life by an accidental overdose to heroin. Her last request was that her heirs bury her body wearing her favorite mink bikini, which she adored.

Brigham Young

June 1, 1801 – August 29, 1877

Brigham Young was a former Governor of the Utah territory and leader of the Church of Latter Day Saints. Young's Will was straight forward leaving around three million in cash and real estate to his family. The strange part was his family. A distribution of his estate occurred between his 16 wives and 46 children.

Peter the Czar
Also known as Peter the Great
June 9, 1672 – February 8, 1725

The Czar ruled Russia from 1682 until his death. In his Will he stated his last wishes to continue to fight the rest of Europe and provided battle plans on how to do so.

T.M. Zink

The Iowa attorney died in 1930. His Last Will and Testament disinherited his wife and daughter, the sum of his estate would invest for 75 years. After said time, the gross amount would be, by his calculations, around four million dollars.

His Will stipulated that the money accumulated would endow the Zink Womanless Library. This would be a Library for men by men. The plan and purpose of the library, spelled out in the Will,

"No woman shall at any time, under any pretense or for any purpose, be allowed inside the library, or upon the premises or have any say about anything concerned therewith, nor appoint any person or persons to perform any act connected therewith."

"No book, work of art, chart, magazine, picture, unless some production by a man, shall be allowed inside or outside the building, or upon the premises, and this shall include all decorations for inside and outside the building."

"There shall be over each entrance to the premises and building a sign in these words: 'No Woman Admitted.'"

"It is my intention to forever exclude all women from the premises and having anything to say or do with the trust estate and library."

Zink described his actions, "My intense hatred of women is not of recent origin or development nor based upon any personal differences I ever had with them but is the result of my experiences with women, observations of them, and study of all literatures and philosophical works within my limited knowledge relating thereto."

The library would have been built in 2006, the end of the 75 years. Lucky for us, after his death, Zink's daughter, Margretta had the Will and Testament overturned due to Zink not being of sound mind during the creation of the document, and the estate given to her.

The Tree that owns itself

Colonel William Henry Jackson cherished his child hood memories of playing on a tree located on his family's property. He desired to protect the tree and deeded the tree and the surrounding land to itself.

"I, W. H. Jackson, of the county of Clarke, of the one part, and the oak tree… of the county of Clarke, of the other part: Witnesseth, That the said W. H. Jackson for and in consideration of the great affection which he bears said tree, and his great desire to see it protected has conveyed, and by these presents do convey unto the said oak tree entire possession of itself and of all land within eight feet of it on all sides."

"Alas, Poor Yorick!"

Some people leave their bodies to help scientific research while others chose to help enhance the arts. A pivotal role in William Shakespeare's Hamlet is that of Yorick, a skull of a friend of the main character.

In 1955, Juan Potomachi promised his estate would give two thousand Pesos to the Buenos Aries Teatro Dramatico with the stipulation that his own skull play the part of Yorick in all productions of Hamlet.

In 1982, Andre Tchaikowsky, polish composer and pianist, died of colon cancer at age 46, in his Will he left his skull to the Royale Shakespeare Society to use as a prop on stage.

John (Pop) Reed left this clause in his will around the mid-19th century

"My head to be separated from my body immediately after my death; the latter to be buried in a grave; the former, duly macerated and prepared, to be brought to the theatre, where I have served all my life, and to be employed to represent the skull of Yorick—and to this end I bequeath my head to the properties."

Unidentified French

The people of France make more of a statement with their Will's.

An unidentified French attorney bequeathed money to an insane asylum. What he called the "local madhouse." His Will stated, "It was simply an act of restitution to his clients."

There was a French doctor who established an annual contest to pick the "Finest nose." Officials of the contest were to not allow any Russians to enter and a required trait would be red hair with black eyebrows.

A French will stipulated that the fortune of the estate would be given to anyone who can claim proof of any message from a higher power.

A French man, who had enough of his own country, requested his heirs donate his estate to feed the poor of England. He then requested them to throw his lifeless body into the waters a mile from the coast of England.

Up High and Down low

A woman in Cherokee County, North Caroline left her estate to God. The judge had to perform his due diligence and ordered the county sheriff to search for the beneficiary. After a few days, the sheriff reported, "after a due and diligent search, God cannot be found in this County."

Earnest Digweed a teacher from England left $26,000 to Jesus Christ, "On the occasion of his return to earth." Provided he could prove his identity, Christ has to return in the next eight years and must return with the goal of reining on earth.

Going in the other direction a man in Finland left his entire estate to the devil. Instead of the local government attempting to search, they took immediate possession of the estate.

3 NON-PROPER DOCUMENTATION

In law school, they teach students to look at the "four corners" of a Will, where you take all the words contained in the entire document and interpret the intent of the deceased. Sometimes, the four corners are not necessarily the four corners of a piece of paper. It can be the bumper of a car, an eggshell, a statute or part of a recipe. In every state of the union, judges will make every effort to admit the Will of a person no matter what material is used. There is a strong public policy in our country that we respect a person's last wishes.

Strange

In an English Probate Court, the estate of a sailor began with a Will written on an eggshell in pencil.

Authorities found a man dead on his couch. He had taken his last moments to write his Will on his shirt along with the names of the people he thought might have killed him.

Francois Rabelais
1494 – April 9, 1553

Rabelais took care of his estate in once sentence, "I have nothing, I owe a great deal, and the rest I leave to the poor."

Karl Tausch

Tausch has the record for the shortest Will in existence. Two words in Latin "Vse Zene," translated, "all to wife."

George Harris

George Harris was a Canadian farmer who had the unfortunate luck of becoming pinned by his tractor. He told everyone he would be out late working. Harris got off the tractor to make some adjustments not knowing that it was in reverse. The tractor backed up and pinned him to another piece of equipment.

Harris fearing the worst used his pocketknife, and etched on the bumper of the tractor, "In case I die in this mess, I leave all to the wife. Cecil Geo Harris."

His family found him at 10:30 pm and they rushed him to the hospital where he died. In order to probate the Will the family had to have the bumper removed and filed with the local courts as Harris' Last Will. The Courts did find the bumper to be a valid Holographic Will and admitted it for probate. The bumper sat in the file room of the courthouse until 1966 when it was transferred to the University of Saskatchewan College of law to be put on display in the library.

"Shoeless" Joe Jackson
July 16, 1887 – December 5, 1951

Jackson was a member of the famous "black sox" team that purposely lost a World Series game. Such actions earned him a lifetime ban from the game of baseball. There was nothing strange written in his Last Will. However, after the death of his wife, two charities, both named beneficiaries of his wife's estate, began a court battle over the actual document that collectors considered sports memorabilia.

Margaret Nothe

Nothe left her Will written on a chili sauce recipe that was accepted into probate.

"Chili Sauce without Working"

4 quarts of ripe tomatoes

4 small onions

4 green peppers

2 teacups of sugar

2 quarts of cider vinegar

2 ounces of all allspice

2 ounces of cloves

2 ounces of cinnamon

12 teaspoons of salt

Chop tomatoes, onions and peppers fine,

The rest mix together and bottle cold

Measure tomatoes when peeled

The Funny Thing About a Will

In case I die before my husband, I leave everything to him.

4 TO MY PETS

For some, pets are like their children and so they have created ways to leave their estates to their beloved pets or animals that have become an important part of the person's life. There are two camps on the estates of the pets. First, are those who consider pets no more than chattel, meaning property, to be left to someone. Second, are the people who leave their pets property. However, pets do not outright receive the funds. They are instead, put in trusts and managed by people who take care of the pet.

Amy Bachman

A San Francisco woman left the vast sums of her estate to The Society for the Prevention of Cruelty to Animals to set up a fund in honor of her dog 'Bingo.' In addition, she left $1.00 to her husband and nothing to her own son.

Elsebeth Christensen

An elderly woman with no living heirs bequeathed six chimps, in Copenhagen Denmark Zoo, around $60,000. Christensen's daughter died from an illness and in the last years of her young life took great joy in visiting the chimps every day. According to Danish law, the Will must be read aloud to all heirs who are named in the Will, a judge stood at the edge of the cage and read the document to the six chimps, Jimmy, Trunte, Fifi, Trine, Grinni, and Gigi. The judge said they behaved better than some of the people, whom he has had to read Wills to, they did not start fighting.

Mr. Garland

A man only identified as Mr. Garland put his pets before his family stating:

"To my monkey, my dear and amusing Jacko, [I leave] the sum of 10 pounds sterling per annum. . . . To my faithful dog Shock, and my well-beloved cat Tibb, a pension of 5 pounds sterling. . . . On the death of all three the sum appropriated to this purpose shall become the property of my daughter Gertrude, to whom I give this preference among my children, because of the large family she has and the difficulty she finds in bringing them up."

Leona Helmsley

July 4, 1920 – August 20, 2007

Nicknamed the "Queen of Mean," Helmsley was an American businesswoman and made her fortune in the hotel industry. She had gained a reputation for take no prisoner tactics with her employees, tenants and even her own family.

When her husband died in 1997, Ms. Helmsley inherited an estate estimated to be worth 5 billion dollars. Ms. Helmsley died of congestive heart failure on August 20, 2007. Her Will had language that wanted to create a twelve million dollar trust fund for her Maltese dog named Trouble. The probate court settled on 2 million dollars, after they thought the original amount was excessive. The dog received $100,000 a year for security, $8,000 a year for grooming and $1,200 a year for food and treats. A $60,000 per year fee goes to the guardian of the dog.

The bulk of her estate established the Leona M. and Harry B. Helmsley Charitable trust and wished that the trust's funds used to benefit dogs. Instead, the trust focused on supporting nonprofit medical research, human services, education, conservatism and the security and development of Israel.

Helmsley also had four grandchildren. She left two a five million dollar trust and five million in cash on the condition that they each visit the grave of their father once a year, and sign a registration book at the grave. Her other two grandchildren were left nothing.

Jonathan Jackson
Died around 1880

Jackson was a lover of all animals especially cats. His Will stated, "it is man's duty to watch over and protect the lesser and feebler." For his part, he left funds for the sole purpose of creating a house for cats. The house was to be a place where cats can enjoy sleeping quarters, dining halls, light conversation in their own rooms and they could dance the night away in an auditorium with a live accordion musician. The installation of specially designed roofs would allow easy climbing as well.

Contessa Carlotta Liebenstein

Died 1991

The Contessa, of German Royalty, left her vast fortune, one hundred and thirty nine million German marks, roughly eighty million U.S. to a single faithful heir, her beloved dog. The Dog, German shepherd named Gunter III. Recently, the funds have transferred to Gunter IV son of Gunter III.

A group, calling themselves the Burgundians, is responsible for the care of Gunther and keeping him and his heir in the life style he has grown accustomed. The dog owns several villas in Italy and a home in the Bahamas.

The fortune has grown to around three hundred million today and the dogs live in the lap of luxury. With house cleaners, limousine and a custom built swimming pool. A few years ago it was reported that the caretakers of Gunther Purchased a palatial eight-bedroom villa in Miami from pop star Madonna. The dog has free reign of the grounds and has taken over Madonna's master bedroom as his own.

Madame Dupis

Madame Dupis died in 1677 leaving behind an allowance of 30 sous per month for food to her two cats. The felines ate meals twice a day, each in their own dish. The meals would consist of a meat soup and soggy bread. She even stated that half the recipe would suffice if one of the cats died.

Alexander McQueen
March 17, 1969 – February 11 2010

Alexander McQueen was a British fashion designer who founded his own label. Lover of pets, McQueen left £100,000 to the Battersea Dogs and Cats Home in south London and set up a £50,000 trust so his own dogs could continue to live in the lifestyle they grew to expect.

Abdel Nahas

Died 1979

Abdel Nahas' best friend was his pet mouse. The mouse died in 1978. Heartbroken Abdel had the mouse mummified so that he could continue to be a part of Nahas life. In 1979, Abdel Nahas died, leaving behind an estate worth around $2 million dollars. His Will left the mouse all of his estate.

Eleanor E. Ritchey

Ritchey was the heir of the Quaker State Refining Corporation. When she died her estate was worth 4.5 million dollars, all of which she left to her 150 dogs. Her family contested the Will, and in 1973, the estate had increased in value to 14 million and the dogs had received 9 million. Only 73 had survived to this date. When the last of the dogs had passed, the trust donated the rest of the funds to the Auburn University Research Foundation for research into canine disease.

Dorothy Roscoe

Roscoe died in 1976 and left $2500 to her friend for the last seventy years, a tortoise named peter. It was her wish that Peter continue to eat strawberries and bananas. In addition, the turtle would continue to have his eyes bathed in milk.

Thomas Shewbridge

Shewbridge looked to take care of his dogs after his death leaving them some $112,000 in 1958. The money bought 29,000 shares of a local power company to which the dogs regularly attended board meetings.

Dusty Springfield
April 16 1939 – March 2 1999

Dusty Springfield was a British singer and record producer, with such hits as, "Wishin and Hopin" and "Preacher Man." She began to take ill in 1994, which would result in her death in 1999. Dusty named her cat as an heir in her Will. The document appointed caretakers of the cat. The cat will only eat imported baby food, have an indoor cat tree, a bed lined with one of Springfield's nightgowns and the cat is allowed to listen only to Springfield songs.

5 REVENGE AND LAST WORDS

Revenge is a dish best served cold. For years people have been leaving the last word of exactly what they thought about their spouses, kids, siblings and whomever the person felt needed to be told off one last time. There are going to be those who suggest strongly that the family left behind will be filled with their grief and guilt from the wrong they inflicted on the departed. However, there is a question about whether the guilt will be enough.

Samuel Bratt

Died 1960

In his life, Samuel Bratt smoked cigars but his wife hated the foul smell and did not allow him to partake. He used the instrument of his Last Will to get a bit of revenge. His estate was valued at £330,000, and he had left this money to his wife under the condition that she must smoke five cigars a day for the rest of her life.

Caroline of Brunswick

Queen of England

May 17, 1768 – August 7, 1821

In life, the King accused the Queen of infidelity. She sought to have the last word on the matter and requested a plaque be affixed to her coffin giving vital statistics and titled her "Outraged Queen of England."

David Davis

An English citizen, who died in 1778, Davis left his wife five shillings "to enable her to get drunk for the last time at my expense."

Philip Grundy

Philip Grundy left everything to his dental assistant on the condition that she would not wear makeup or see other men for at least five years after his death.

Adolph J. Heimbeck
Died 1958

Adolph J. Heimbeck decided to let his sisters know his dissatisfaction with their political views.

"I leave nothing to my two sisters Hazel and Katherine as they revered Franklin D. Roosevelt and the taxes caused by him more than equaled their share."

Heinrich Heine
December 13, 1797 – February 17, 1856

Heine was a famous poet, known for his poems dedicated to his beloved wife. In 1848, he suddenly found himself paralyzed and confined to what he called his "Mattress Grave." During this time, the attentions of Heine fell upon Camille Selden, who would visit him regularly.

In his Will Heine left his entire fortune to his wife, on the condition that she had to remarry. It was Heine's hope "there will be at least one man to regret my death."

Mary Kuhery

Mary Kuhery left her loving husband $2.00 under the condition that he would go out and purchase a rope to hang himself.

Francis R. Lord

Lord was a citizen of Australia, who left only one shilling to his wife along with instructions that she use the shilling "for tram fare so she could go somewhere and drown herself." Mrs. Lord never claimed her inheritance.

S.A. Mike

A Nigerian civil servant wished to express his revenge and have the last laugh on his family members in his Will. Mike wrote to his wife, "to my beloved wife I leave you with your lover with the knowledge that I wasn't the fool you thought I was." Then he stated, "To my son I leave my cars which you almost ruined and I want you to have the satisfaction of finishing the job."

Anthony Scott

Anthony Scott Wrote In his Will, "to my first wife Sue, whom I always promised to mention in my will. 'Hello Sue!'"

Garvey B. White
Died 1908

Before any estate business in his Will, Garvey B. White stated fifty cents would be paid to his son-in-law, "to enable him to buy a good stout rope with which to hang himself. And thus rid mankind of one on the most infamous scoundrels."

6 IGNORED LAST WISHES

There are cases where the beneficiaries ignored the last wishes of the departed. There are Wills that refer to an inventory or letter incorporated in the Will and made a part of it. However, these items are rarely found and sometimes located after the terms of the Will have been admitted or carried out. Some requests are too difficult for the family members to carry out and they ignore the requests not out of spite but out of respect to the loved one. Whatever the reason, ignored last wishes do occur and often do cause conflict and hurt feelings to those who believe that executors should carry out and respect them.

Princess Diana of Wales

July 1, 1961 – August 31, 1997

In addition to her will, Princess Diana left a letter of wishes to detail the further distribution of her estate to her seventeen godchildren. She wished one quarter of her personal items distributed amongst her godchildren, but her executors ignored her request and hid the letter. It would remain hidden if not for the trial of her butler who was stealing possession from the estate.

Charles Dickens

February 7, 1812 – June 9, 1870

Known for such literary works as, A Tale of Two Cities, David Copperfield and A Christmas Carol, Dickens was one of few authors of the time who knew fame and fortune while he was still alive. He tried to live a modest life and why would his Will be any different? He asked that no one be allowed to wear black at his funeral. He wanted eternal rest at Rochester Cathedral "in an inexpensive, unostentatious, and strictly private manner," asking that the date and time be kept secret from the public so that none of his fans would attend.

His heirs ignored his wishes and laid him to rest in the poet's corner or Westminster Abbey with all the pomp and circumstance of a grand funeral procession.

Marilyn Monroe
June 1, 1926 – August 15, 1962

Born Norma Jean Morteson, Monroe took Hollywood by storm. She starred in mainstream movies, stole the heart of a President and is the role model for young starlets in Hollywood today. In 1962, authorities found Monroe dead in her California home.

In her Will, she left her personal effects, including jewelry, clothing, shoes and undergarments to Lee Strasberg. Monroe wished Strasberg would distribute them amongst her friends and family. Instead, Strasberg stored everything in a warehouse, which he left to his widow after his death. The Widow Strasberg had the items auctioned off.

Publius Vergilius Maro

Also known as "Virgil"

70 BC- 19 BC

Virgil wished to create a story that experts consider on the same level as Homers The Iliad and The Odyssey.

Not satisfied with the editing of the epic, Virgil traveled to Greece where he could spend some time to perform a final revision. In his travels, Virgil caught a fever and grew deathly ill. Before his death, he asked his literary executors Lucius Varius Rufus and Plotius Tucca to burn the original draft of the epic. With only small corrections left to make, Virgil felt he would rather have his masterpiece burned than published unfinished.

The emperor Agustus, who had originally commissioned the Aenied, ordered the executors to ignore Virgil's last request and publish the Aenied with few editorial changes.

7 OOPS, I FORGOT

A Will can cost anywhere from $200-1200, depending on the particular attorney, or whether you wish to do it yourself. However, hundreds of people die each day without a Will and the ramifications of doing so increase the cost, especially for those who die leaving money.

Countless celebrities whose worth was in the millions, when they died, did not take the time to get a Will prepared. Why? Their estates have paid dearly in taxes. The reality is that individual states will create a Will for a person who dies without the document. In reality, no one ever dies without a Will. What the deceased gives up is control of their estate. All heirs receive an equal share regardless of the relationship.

James Brown

May 3, 1933 – December 25, 2006

James Brown was an American musical icon. Brown had earned the title The Godfather of Soul. his Will names six of his seven children. In addition, the document did not mention his new wife, Tomi Rae Hynie. Brown signed the Will six years before his death, ten months before the birth of his son, James II, and more than a year before his marriage to Hynie.

Hynie filed a lawsuit against the estate asking the court to recognize her as the widow, and appoint a special administrator to be in charge of the estate. Claims surfaced that Hynie and Brown were separated at the time, however under South Carolina law, where the Will was probated, a wife and child of a relationship are entitled to inheritance as long as they are not disinherited in the Will

Chief Justice Warren Burger

September 17, 1907 – June 25, 1995

Burger was the 15th Chief Justice of the United State Supreme Court, who ruled on such decisions as abortion, school desegregation, and capital punishment. However, when he died, he disposed of his entire estate in only one hundred seventy-six words. He failed leave the executors a grant of powers and did not provide language that would deal with estate taxes, costing his heirs extra attorney fees.

Heath Ledger

April 4, 1979 – January 22, 2008

Mr. Ledger was an Australian actor of immense talent, who won the Academy Award for best actor in a supporting role, posthumously, for his role as the Joker in The Dark Knight. A housekeeper discovered his body in his apartment in New York. Ledger left behind a fortune of twenty million dollars, and a two-year-old daughter name Matlida Rose.

Unfortunately, Ledger did not have the time to update his Will. After his death, a produced Will named his parents and his siblings as heirs. The division of his estate would be between them. This was an old document written before the birth of his daughter. Another Will emerged, that was updated with the names of his daughter but Mr. Ledger had yet to sign it. Fortunately, his parents knew what their son would have wanted, and they gifted 16 million to their grandchild as her inheritance from her father.

Anna Nicole Smith

November 28, 1964 – February 8, 2007

No other celebrity had her affairs intertwined with probate court than Smiths. The court battles began with her marriage to one J. Howard Marshall, a 90-year-old Texas oilman. Smith said it was true love, while others though it was gold digging.

Marshall Died on August 4, 1995. He left behind a Will and Trust that excluded Anna Nicole Smith. A court battle ensued in multiple jurisdictions, including the federal court. She argued that Marshall had orally agreed to place her in his estate plan. The proceedings would take in excess of ten years.

Right after the birth of her daughter, Smith's son, Daniel, died in 2006. He was visiting his mother and new sister in the hospital when he passed away. After an informal commitment ceremony with her attorney Howard K. Stern, not a marriage, Anna Nicole Smith herself passed away.

A judge ordered her heirs to produce Smiths Will. The Document listed that Howard K. Stern hold her entire estate in trust for her son Daniel, and excluded any other children. The language was ruled outdated and named her daughter the heir of the estate.

In 2011, the court ruled that the estate of Anna Nicole Smith was entitled to funding from the estate of J. Howard Marshall, last ordered around the tune of 50 million dollars. Howard K. Stern manages the trust for Smith's daughter through her guardian, Larry Birkhead.

CELEBRITIES WHO HAVE DIED WITHOUT A WILL

Jimmy Hendrix
November 27, 1942 – September 18, 1970

The legal battle over his estate went on for nearly thirty years. At stake were the royalties and ownership on the rights of his music that continue to generate revenue.

Amy Winehouse
September 14, 1983 – July 23, 2011

Her parents claimed Amy's estate, roughly worth a bit less than 5 million. Under British law, they were they were her closest living heirs since she died without a Will.

Bob Marley

February 6, 1945 – May 11 1981

Dozens of claimants stepped forward to try to get a piece of the thirty million dollar estate. His music continues to generate funds to this date.

Barry White

September 12, 1944 – July 4, 2003

Left behind one ex-wife, one wife and one longtime girlfriend all with children from the singer to fight over his established estate and any future money from royalties.

Jill Dando

November 9, 1961 – April 16, 1999

A BBC journalist who died by gunshot, outside her home, without a Will. Her father inherited her estate.

Salvatore Philip "Sonny" Bono

February 16, 1935 – January 5, 1998

Sonny died in a skiing accident, and both current wife and ex-wife Cher laid claims against the estate. In addition, a person claiming to be the illegitimate son of Bono brought forth a claim.

Karl Stig-Erland "Stieg" Larsson

August 15, 1954 – November 9, 2004

When the author, of The Girl with the Dragon Tattoo, died his father claimed the estate leaving Larson's longtime partner with nothing. Eventually the father gave the property that the two shared to him, but none of the royalties associated with his books.

Roman Blum

Blum had the distinct misfortune to die without a Will and without an heir. The city of New York is holding his estate in the hopes that a genealogical search can help find an heir.

Pablo Picasso

October 25, 1881 – April 8, 1973

Picasso died with an estate that may have ranged from $100 to $260 million dollars. No one located a Will. After six years that cost the estate $30 million dollars, which ended in the assets being divided between his six living heirs. The family still fights over merchandising rights of the name Picasso.

Tupac Shakur

June 16, 1971 – September 13, 1996

One of the more active estates in history, bringing in millions every year since he died, and thanks to modern technology Shakur is still making concert appearance. Shakur died without a Will. His mother filed the papers creating the estate of Tupac Shakur, which sees revenues of $15 million a year.

Paul Shane

June 19, 1940 – May 16, 2013

A British comedian who died without a Will left his daughters to work on his estate.

Adam Michael Goldstein "DJ AM"

March 30, 1973 – August 28, 2009

DJ AM died with no Will. Fortunately, he died with no children and no relationships. It was easy for his mother to claim to his estate.

Steve McNair

February 14, 1973 – July 4, 2009

The famous quarterback died leaving behind a twenty million dollar estate. Upon death, the Probate Court froze the funds of the estate pending a $4 million dollar tax payment.

Howard Hughes, Jr.

December 24, 1905 – April 5, 1976

After Hughes' death, the search began for any sign of a Will. Many were surprised to find out that a Will found, by a random stranger, in the Mormon Church headquarters in Utah. However, experts proved the document a forgery and the Court divided the 2.2 billion estate amongst his twenty-two cousins.

John Denver

December 31, 1943 – October 12, 1997

John Denver died in a plane crash without a Will. The courts took six years to work out a settlement in the estate for his heirs.

8 BATTLE FOR THE ESTATE

Death is a heartfelt time of remembrance and joy. Funerals are also breeding grounds for gossip, drama and backstabbing. I have seen families fight over a tablecloth that the mother used once at a Thanksgiving dinner twenty years ago. Can you imagine the fights that occur in estates worth millions? Heirs will come out of the woodwork for a share and funeral is usually the first sign of the green-eyed monster.

I frequently refer to a "death race," where family members race to the home of the deceased to loot property. In other cases there have been estates that have well written Wills, but that will not stop greedy individuals from filing lawsuits looking for their perceived fair share.

Gary Coleman

February 8, 1968 – May 28, 2010

Coleman began acting at a young age, with his own television series. After the series ended, legal, financial and health troubles began to fill his life. On May 26, 2010, a hospital admitted Colman after falling down the stairs and hitting his head. Doctors put him on life support until he died, two days later at the age of 42.

Immediately after his death, disputes over his estate began to disrupt the funeral itself. Authorities later claimed that his ex-wife discontinued the life support and may not have had the authority to do so, but the hospital revealed that Coleman did have an Advanced Health Care Directive giving his ex-wife the power to make such medical decision.

Colman left multiple Wills, with the last naming his business associate, Anna Gray, as executor and awarded the entire estate to her. However, Coleman's ex-wife claimed in court that even though they were divorced, both she and Coleman were living in a common-law relationship, sharing a home and bank accounts. The court ruled that the ex-wife did not meet the requirements for the state of Utah's common law marriage and could not be an heir of the estate.

Doris Duke

November 22, 1912 – October 28, 1993

Duke was an American heir of the tobacco tycoon James Buchanan Duke. In her life, she gave birth to only one child, who died a day after the birth. In her later years, she legally adopted a woman named Chandi Heffner, whom Duke claimed was the reincarnation of her deceased child. However, before her death, they had a falling out. Duke changed her Will and expressed her wishes that Heffner not inherit from the two trusts set up by Dukes father, and in essence negated the adoption.

Duke had left almost all her fortune to several charities already existing and a few the document would create. The Will also appointed her butler Bernard Lafferty as the executor. Accountants estimated Dukes estate worth at $1.3 billion, and many heirs filed lawsuits to contest the Will. An executor, named in a previous version of the Will, claimed that Lafferty tricked, a sick, Duke into signing a new Will. A nurse who was with Duke at the end that claimed Lafferty and a physician attempted to expedite the death of Duke.

Duke's Will carried an "interrorm clause" that said if any

beneficiary, who disputed the Will's provisions would receive nothing, but that did not stop Duke University from filing a lawsuit saying it was entitled to more than the ten million left to them.

In the end, all the lawsuits tied up the estate for nearly three years. The courts eventually removed the butler as executor after they proved he used estate funds for his own support. They then appointed a new executor and trustees. All together, the Duke estate paid ten million in legal fees.

W.C. Fields

January 29, 1880 – December 25, 1946

Fields was an American actor known by all moviegoers for the catch phrase, "my little Chickadee." Fields died from a stomach hemorrhage on Christmas day, a holiday he despised. A clause in his Will stated that an orphanage was to be set up "where no religion of any sort is preached." His wife and son contested the clause.

Vast sums of money were unaccounted for in Field's estate. He had placed certain funds in banks and never kept a written record. Today there could still be accounts accumulating interest unknown to the heirs.

Jerome John "Jerry" Garcia

August 1, 1942 – August 9, 1995

Jerry Garcia was the lead singer for the band, The Grateful Dead. In his Will, he had a section dedicated to his guitars, special made by one man.

"I give all my guitars made by DOUGLAS ERWIN, to DOUGLAS ERWIN, or to his estate if he predeceases me."

The rest of The Grateful Dead thought the guitars in question were actually property of the band. A lawsuit began between the two parties. In 2001 a judge ruled in favor of Erwin upholding the Will of Jerry Garcia.

Groucho Marx

October 2, 1980 – August 19, 1977

Groucho was an American comedian, star of movies and television. Moviegoers recognize his moustache cigar and glasses, today around the world. In the early seventies, he had met a young woman, Erin Fleming, who helped launch the elderly Groucho back into the spotlight.

After his death, a court battle ensued between Fleming and

Groucho's son over the estate. Other celebrities, such as George Burns, came to testify in in favor of Fleming. At one point, during the trial, Fleming assaulted a bailiff with her purse. In the end, the judge ruled that Fleming had to repay the estate the money that she had taken.

Nina Wang

September 13, 1937 – April 3, 2007

Wang became Asia's richest woman with a net worth of around 4 billion dollars. After her death, two Wills surfaced. One written in 2002, giving the bulk of money in the estate to her charitable trust, the other written in 2006 named her Feng Shui decorator as the sole beneficiary. A lengthy court battle ensued and experts discovered that the 2006 Will was a forgery. The court upheld the 2002 Will and awarded the estate to the charitable trust. The decorator planned to appeal, but authorities arrested him the next day on suspicion of forgery.

Dennis Hopper

May 17, 1936 – May 29, 2010

Dennis Hopper was an American actor. He died from advanced prostate cancer that had spread to his bones. At the time of his death, Hopper was in the process of divorcing his fifth wife, Victoria Duffy.

Duffy claimed her rights as a spouse, and used her prenuptial agreement, which spelled out a payment in the event of Hoppers death if they were still married. The Estate is still unsettled between Duffy and Hopper's children.

9 AFTERWORD

I have nothing but the utmost respect for those who have died and attempted to put their affairs in order. My hobby has been to research those Wills written by others so that I can do a better job for those I represent. Wills come in all shapes, and sizes

People collect possessions all through their life that require disposal after death, and as hard as we may try in life, we cannot take it with us. Some, like my mother, will choose a standard Will to leave their property to loved ones. Others, like many in this book, will get creative with their Last Will and Testament.

Dying without a Will of any kind will cause more grief and costs than had the person died with a Will. In my years of practice, I have heard many reasons for not having a Will.

"I just wrote what I want down on some paper and signed it."

Well, another family member, who you might dislike, has another piece of paper leaving everything to him and this document appears to be signed by you as well. Even though it might be a forgery, are you still around to discredit his claim.

"I do not like to think about dying." I know that sometimes it is hard to confront our own mortality, but sit through a probate hearing one afternoon at your local courthouse. Look at the faces of the family members left behind spending months trying to clean up a mess you made by dying without a Will. In addition, the cost of getting a Will is far cheaper than dying without one.

"I do not need one, my family knows what I want and will honor my wishes." Do they really know what you want? Have you remarried? Do you have children from previous relationships? A Will guarantees that your property will go to the individuals you choose, in the manner you specify. If you die without a Will, most states have laws that will write one for the departed. You might not like who stands in line to get your property.

"My kids can work it out themselves." Remember that family vacation you took, with your children in the back seat, the constant back and forth yelling between your children "he won't stop looking at me," "make him stop." Think of this when you decide that your children are able to work it out themselves.

"I am Afraid of Lawyers." Most of us will not bite and, in fact, can be quite entertaining.

"I have no one to leave my property." Through a Will you can leave your property to whoever or whatever you wish, including neighbors, friends, charities, schools, universities or churches and in some cases your pets.

"I am too young and will not need one until I have kids." The fact is that the moment you buy furniture, cars and real estate, you accumulate property. This property needs to be given away after you die. Some of that property requires transferring title and the easiest and less costly way to transfer that title is through a Will.

"I plan on taking it all with me." The likelihood of your heirs burying you with the Mercedes and your guitar is not likely to occur unless you leave a Will.

"I will get to it tomorrow." This is the most common answer and tomorrow you might die in a car accident. Attorneys can draft a Will rather quickly.

People will convince themselves with any excuse, and it is

unfortunate because the world is full of loved ones saying, "If they only had a Will." With only a few sheets of paper that take care of your family, you will sleep easier at night.

If you already have a Will, congratulations, but now you have a duty to keep it updated. Are your named executors and beneficiaries the same today as they were when you had the Will drafted? I suggest you have an attorney look over your Will every three to five years or after what I refer to as "triggering event." Deaths, divorces, births and adoptions are triggering events that may call for an update to your Will.

Finally, take a hard look at all you have accumulated throughout your lifetime and think about those you will leave behind. Are there any last words you wish to convey to them to let them know from beyond the grave? There is nothing preventing you from going outside the scope of the normal Will and leaving something behind that is just a little bit different from everyone else.

ABOUT THE AUTHOR

"The Funny Thing About a Last Will" is Donna Broom's first book. She has been writing since her grandmother gave her first journal at age nine. Thirty years ago, she began collecting wills from probate courts and public records from all over the world. Some of her exciting world travels included touring Cuba as a family law delegate, where she smoked A cigar with Fidel Castro and partied with the Buena Vista Social Club. She also traveled by cattle truck through the mountains of Nicaragua providing medical care to women, children and found herself assisting doctors to deliver babies in the dark, while guerillas exchanged gunfire. Everywhere she would go, Donna collected stories told to her by attorneys, judges, clerks and some everyday people about strange Last Will and Testaments.

Donna Broom is a practicing attorney, in the areas of Last Wills and Testaments, probate and family law. She taught law school for five years, Her education includes a JD, BS in Psychology and Anthropology and PhD. in Clinical Psychology.